D0503911

BELMONT AVENUE

Music by ALAN MENKEN
Lyrics by GLENN SLATER

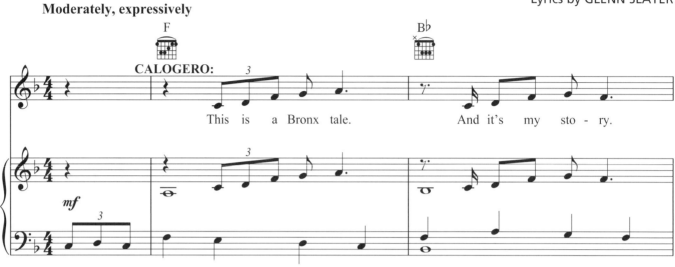

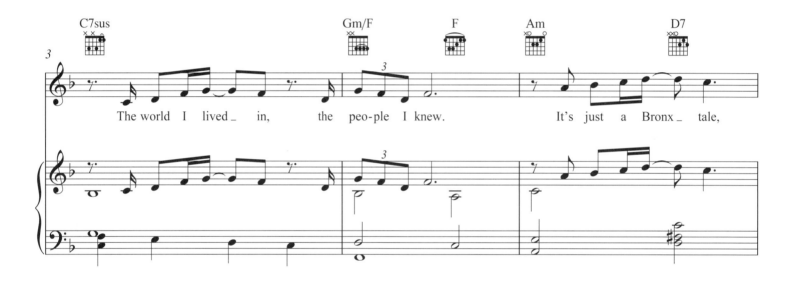

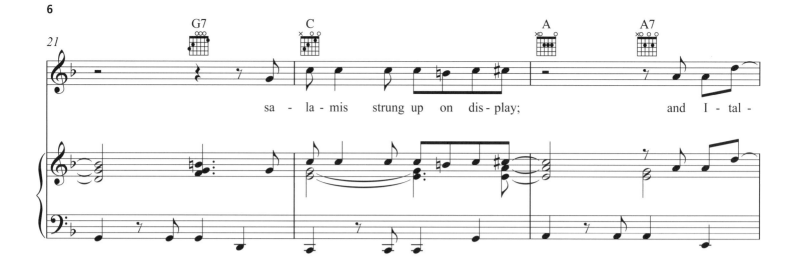

sa - la - mis strung up on dis - play; and I - tal -

- ians are all____ that you see. (Yeah, yeah, and the side - walk's swing - in'!

Yeah, yeah, and the girls____ are sing - in' shoop, shoop,...)

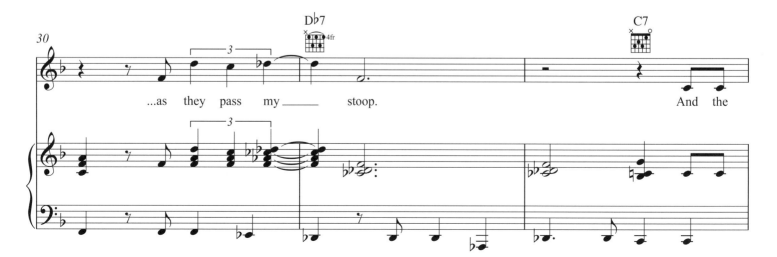

...as they pass my_____ stoop. And the

push-cart ped-dlers, they hawk their wares door to door,

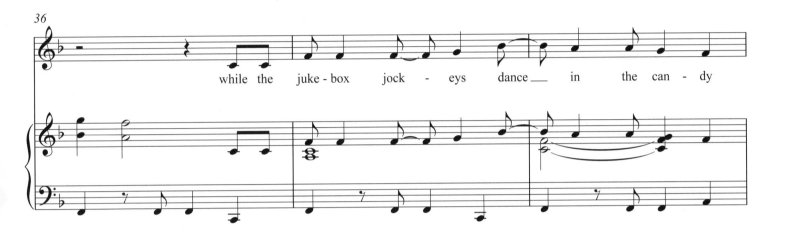

while the juke-box jock-eys dance in the can-dy

store.

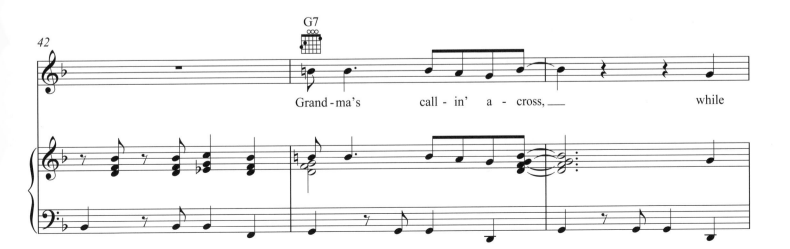

Grand-ma's call-in' a-cross, while

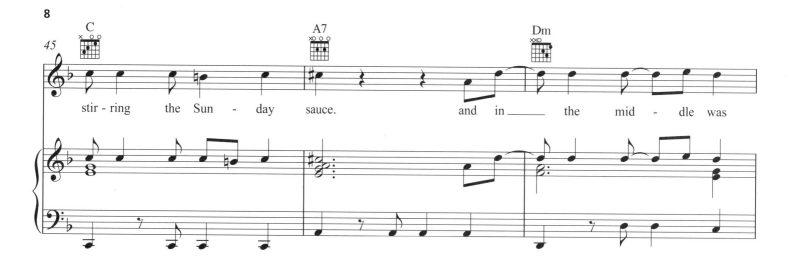

stir - ring the Sun - day sauce. and in ____ the mid - dle was

me. (Whoa, whoa, and the street ___ starts sigh - in'. Whoa, whoa, when the girls _

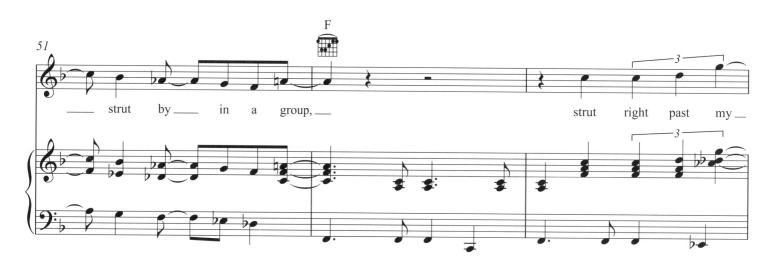

___ strut by ___ in a group, ___ strut right past my _

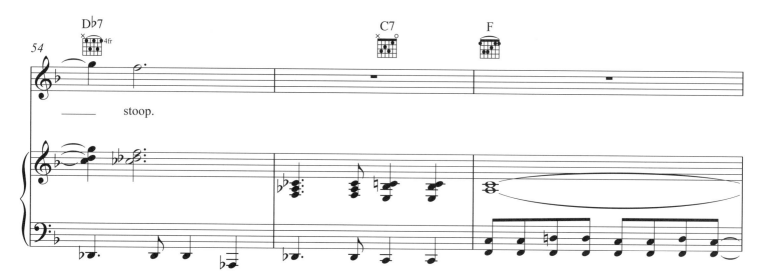

___ stoop.

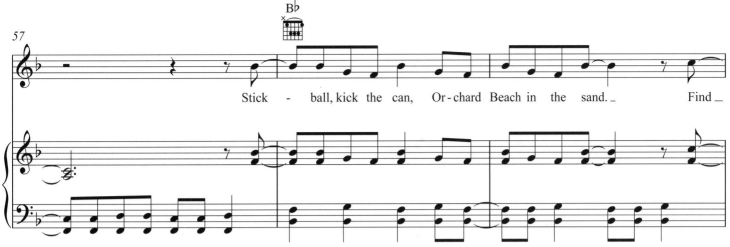

Stick - ball, kick the can, Or - chard Beach in the sand. ___ Find ___

___ a girl and cop a feel. ___ Bryl - creem, ___ wet dream, ___ bring ___

___ her home and close the deal. (No, no, no. No, no, no. No, no, no. ___ Next ___

___ year's Frank - ie Val - lie's croon - in' in the al - leys, get - tin' those fal - set - tos to soar, ___

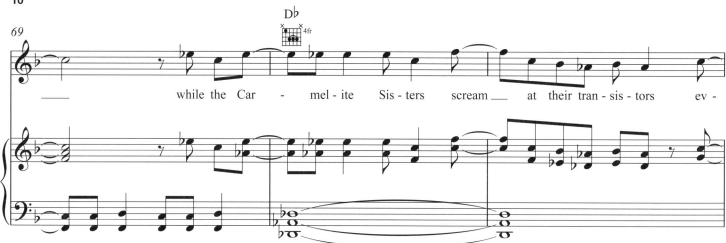

while the Car - mel - ite Sis - ters scream ___ at their tran - sis - tors ev -

- 'ry time the Bomb - ers ___ score! ___

Hang - in' with the crew, (On the stoop, on the

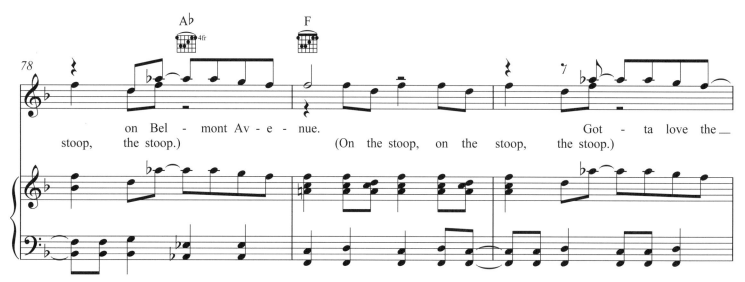

stoop, the stoop.) (On the stoop, on the stoop, the stoop.)

on Bel - mont Av - e - nue. Got - ta love the ___

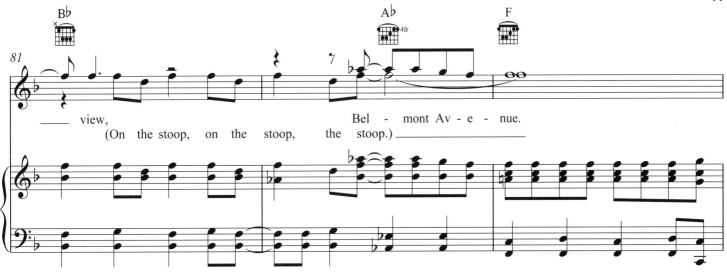

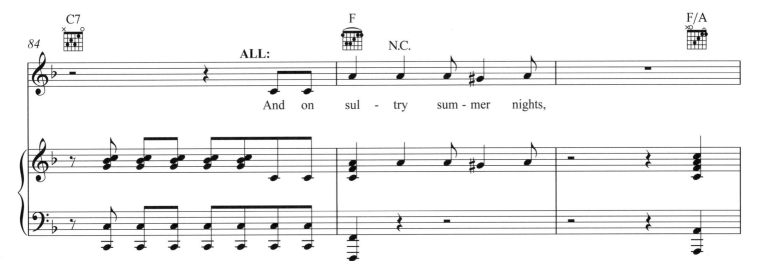

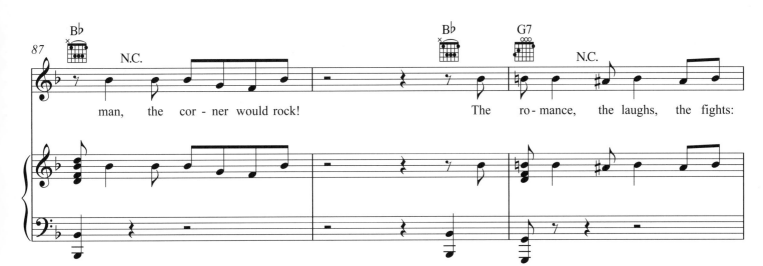

'Eh, _____ oh. _____ Ev - 'ry - where, ev -

'ry - where! I go!

WOMEN:
Bel - mont Av - e - nue! Yeah, yeah, and the noise is grow - in'!

CALOGERO & MEN:
Bel - mont Av - e - nue! Hang - in' with my ___

Half as fast

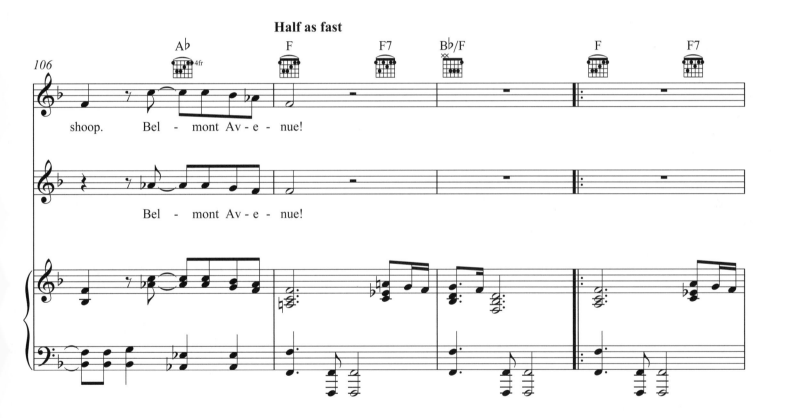

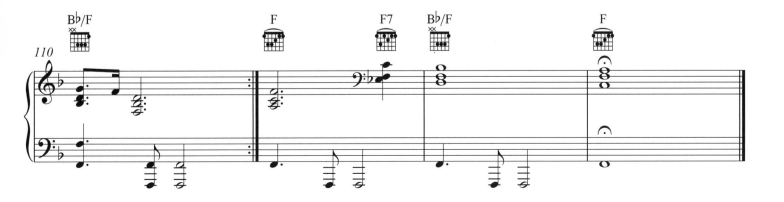

LOOK TO YOUR HEART

Music by ALAN MENKEN
Lyrics by GLENN SLATER

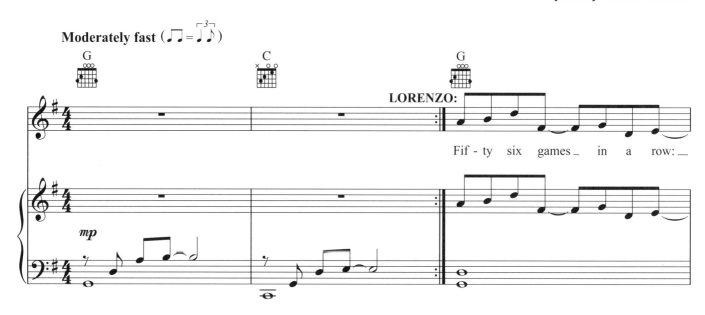

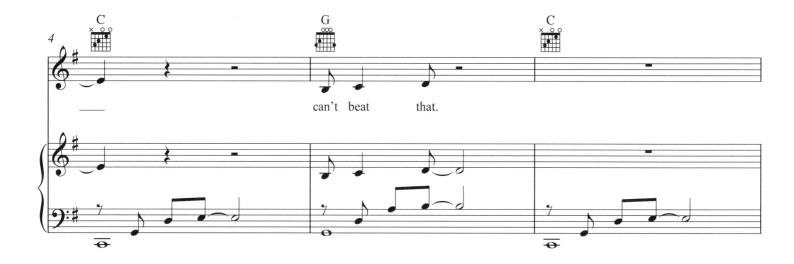

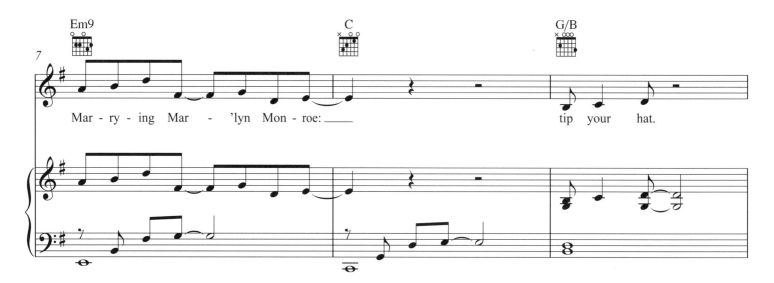

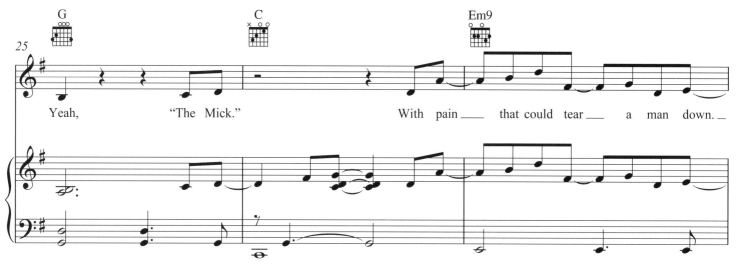

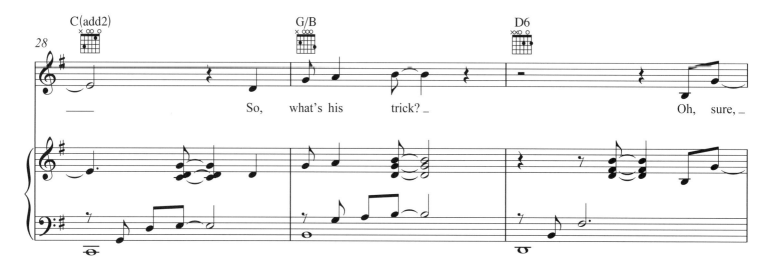

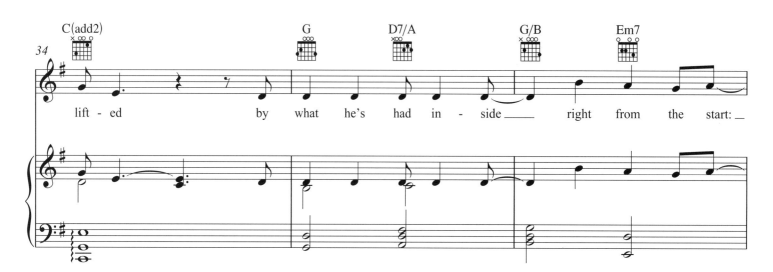

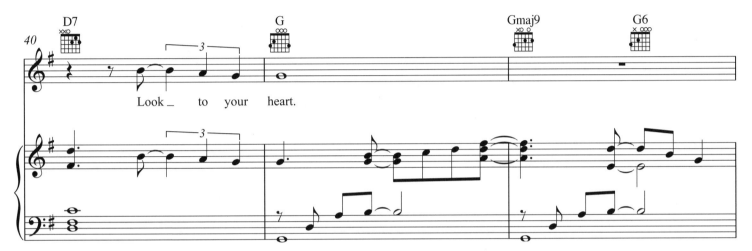

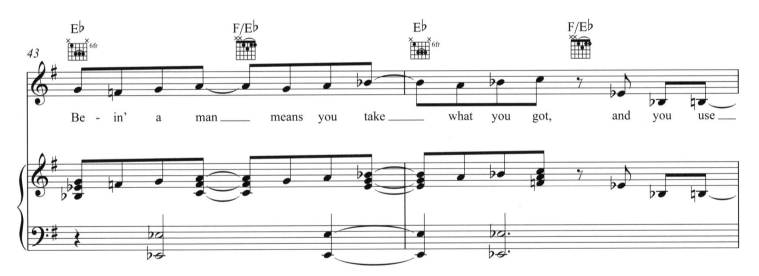

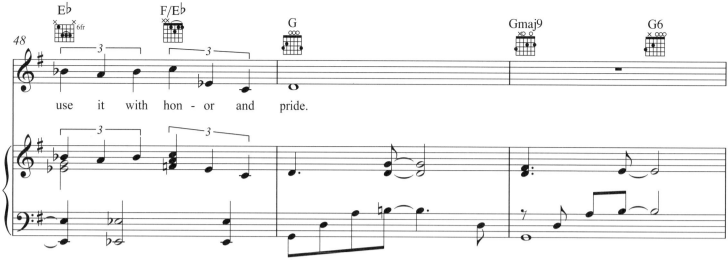

48

use it with hon - or and pride.

51

Some-bod - y shows_ you a short - cut, you smile and re - fuse it.

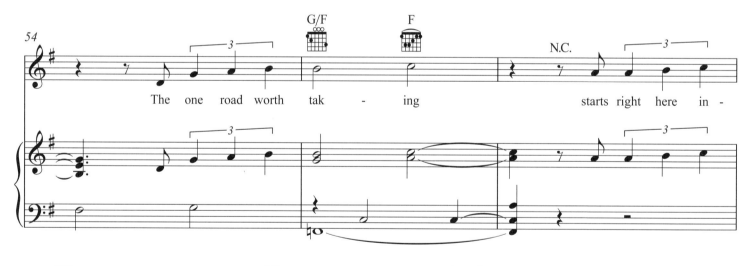

54

The one road worth tak - ing starts right here in -

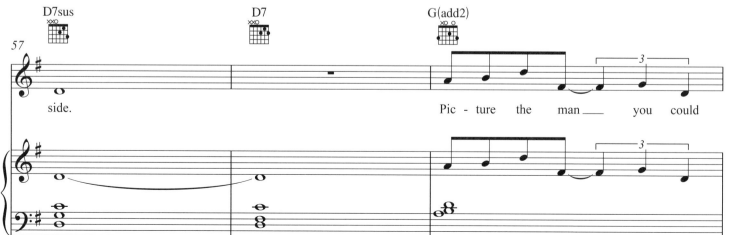

57

side. Pic - ture the man_ you could

be, then aim true. If you get lost, look to

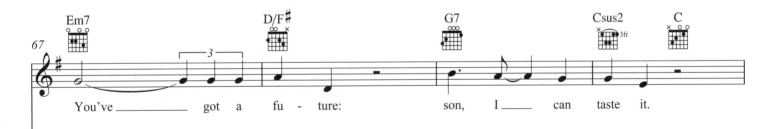

me: I'm here for you. ___

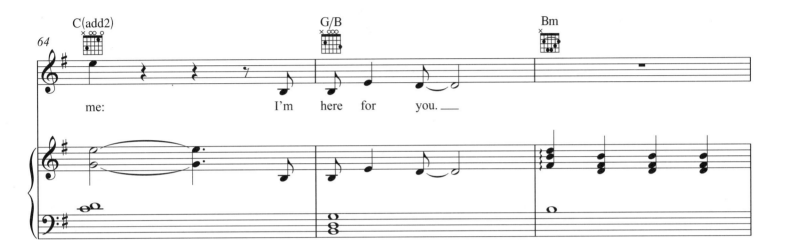

You've ___ got a fu - ture: son, I ___ can taste it.

You ___ can be an - y - thing ___ once you've em -

ROLL 'EM

Music by ALAN MENKEN
Lyrics by GLENN SLATER

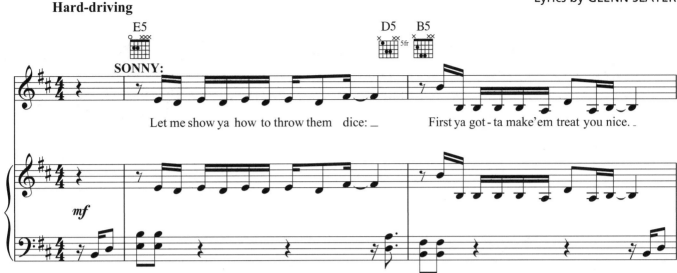

Let me show ya how to throw them dice: __ First ya got - ta make 'em treat you nice. __

Here's a lit - tle bit of free ad - vice: __ lis - ten to Son - ny, we'll __ make some mon - ey.

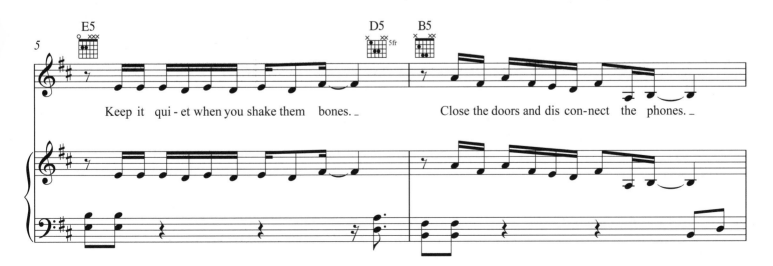

Keep it qui - et when you shake them bones. __ Close the doors and dis con - nect the phones. __

24

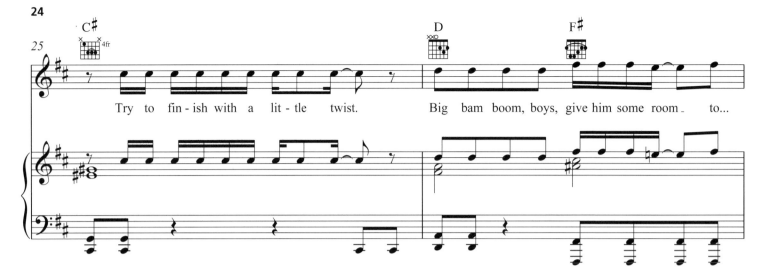

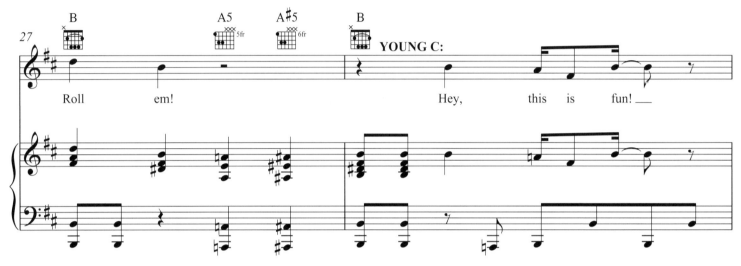

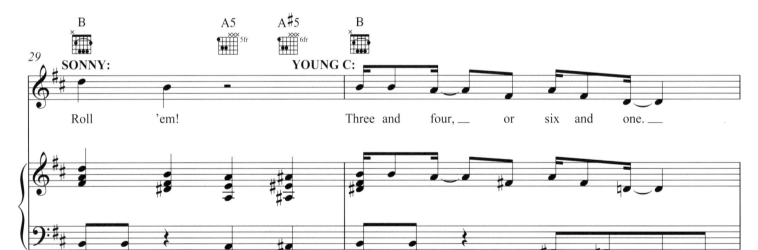

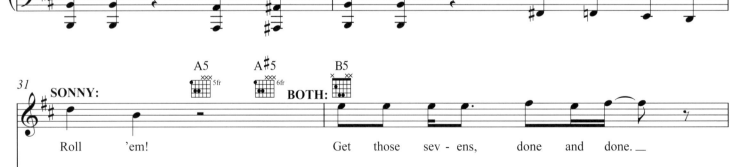

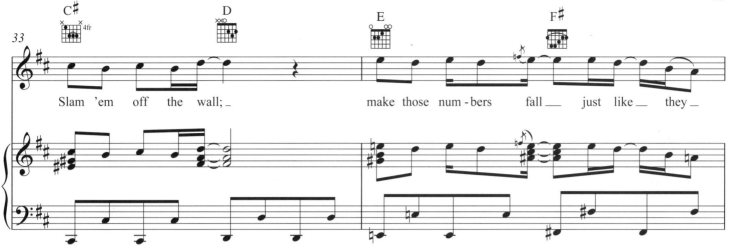

Slam 'em off the wall; ___ make those num-bers fall ___ just like ___ they ___

should.

SONNY: DON'T roll a sev-en. We're this ___ close to heav-en. We'll be ___ in the mon-ey un-less ___ you crap out.

Box-cars, snake eyes: that's all it-'ll take, ___ guys, the kid is a hon-ey, he'll do it, no doubt. ___

I LIKE IT

Music by ALAN MENKEN
Lyrics by GLENN SLATER

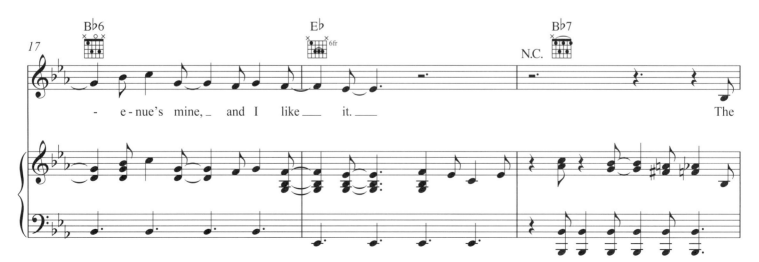

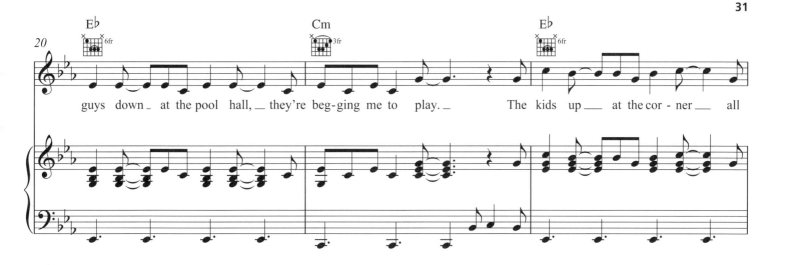

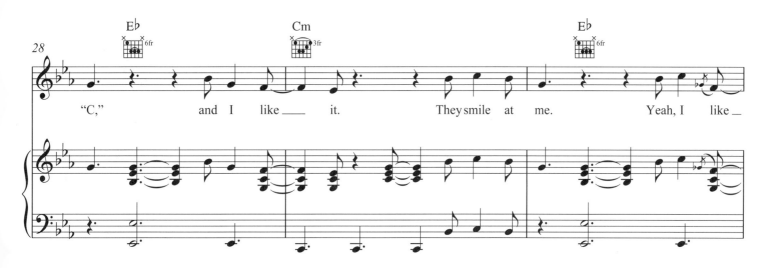

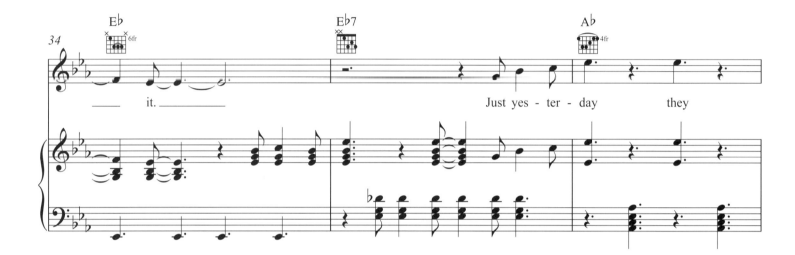

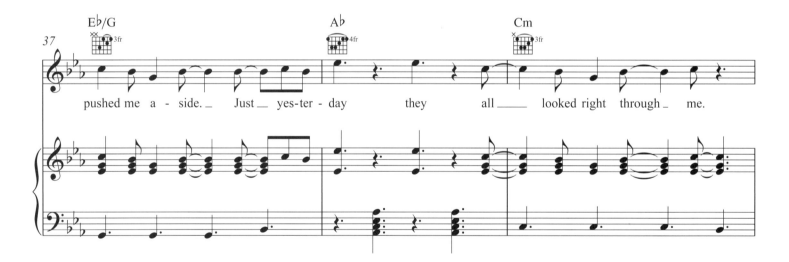

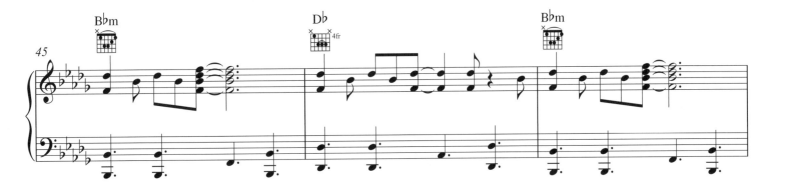

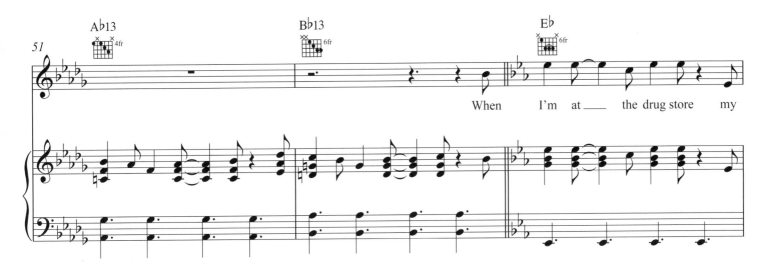

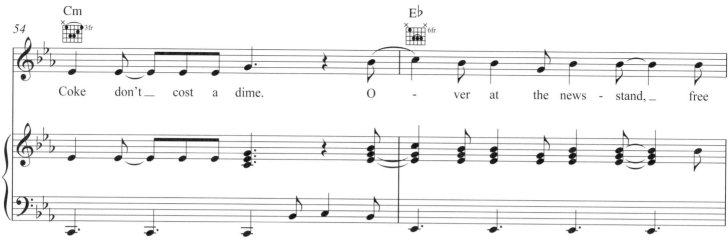

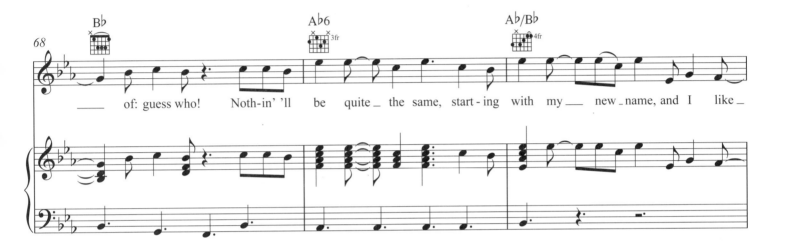

AIN'T IT THE TRUTH

Music by ALAN MENKEN
Lyrics by GLENN SLATER

(yeah). You put on the fe - do - ra, the so - phis - ti - cat - ed au - ra, and you

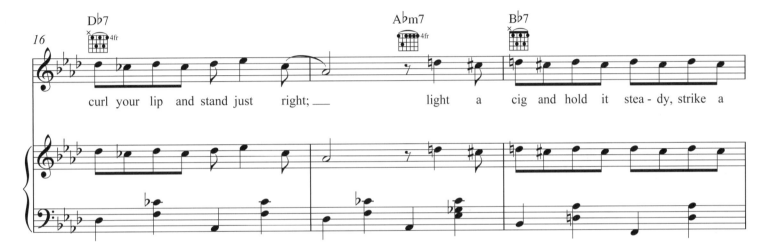

curl your lip and stand just right; ___ light a cig and hold it stea - dy, strike a

pose, and now you're read - y to hang on the cor - ner all night. (Ain't it the

truth?) You know ___ it. Ev - 'ry word is true. (Ain't it the truth?) You lis - ten what I'm

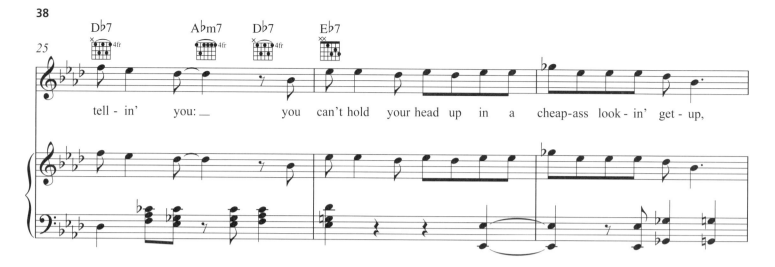

tell-in' you: ___ you can't hold your head up in a cheap-ass look-in' get-up,

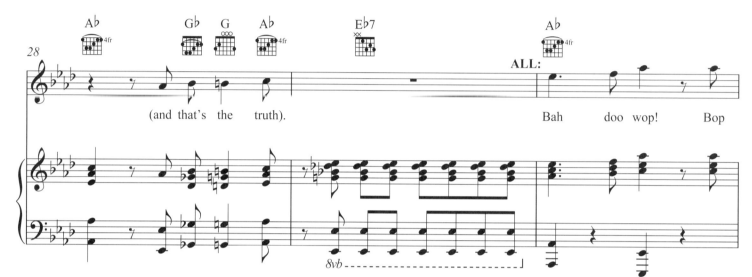

(and that's the truth). ALL: Bah doo wop! Bop

bop ba-dah, dah. Bah doo wop! Sha sha shoo-wah dah!

Bah doo wop! Bop bop ba-dah, dah. Bop bop ba-da-da-dow. ___

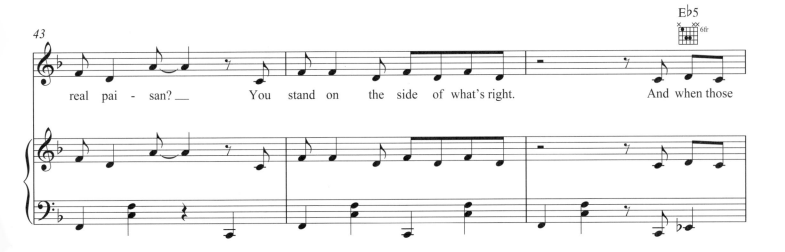

al-ways heard. _ The next tribe that pass-es, you can bet we'll kick their ass-es,

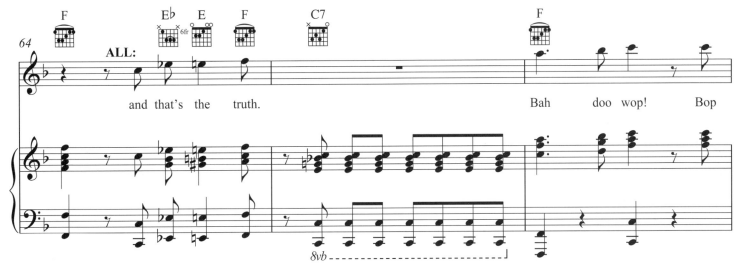

ALL: and that's the truth. Bah doo wop! Bop

bop ba-dah, dah. Bah doo wop! Sha sha shoo wah dah! Bah doo wop! Bop

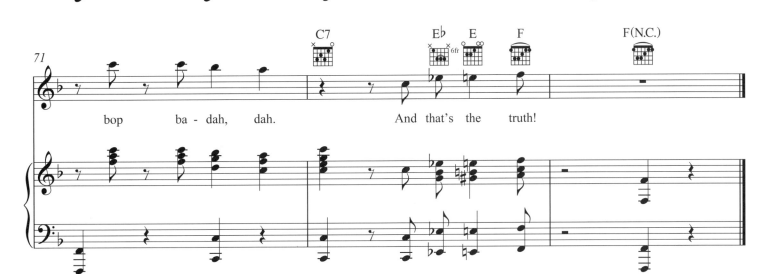

bop ba-dah, dah. And that's the truth!

OUT OF YOUR HEAD

Music by ALAN MENKEN
Lyrics by GLENN SLATER

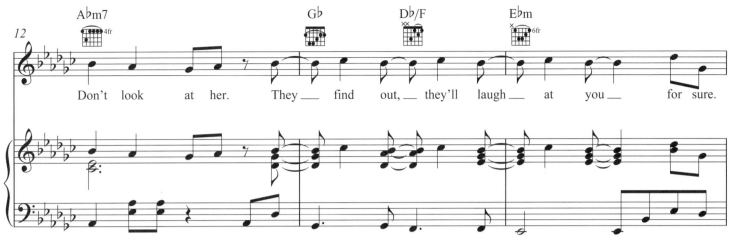

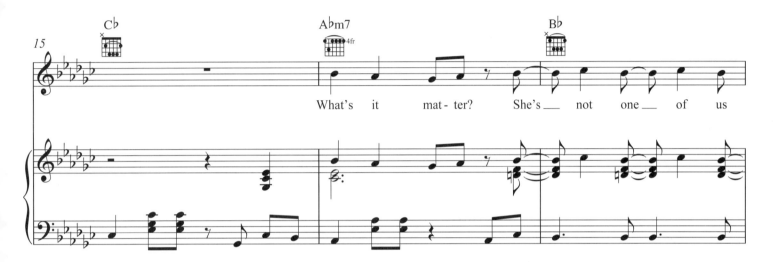

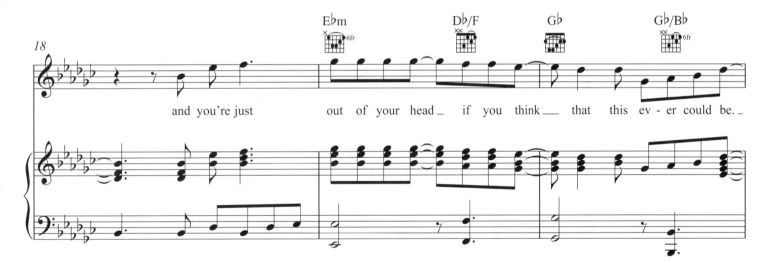

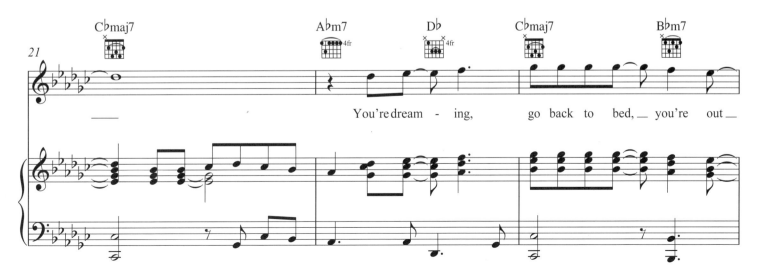

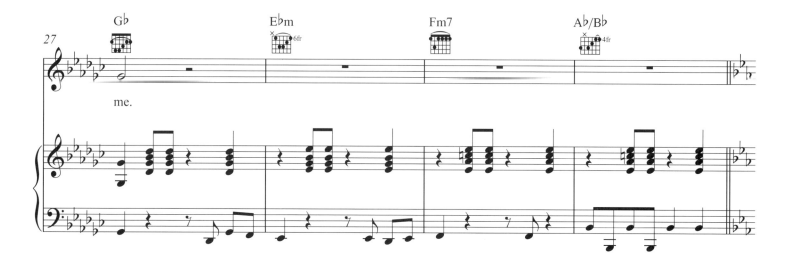

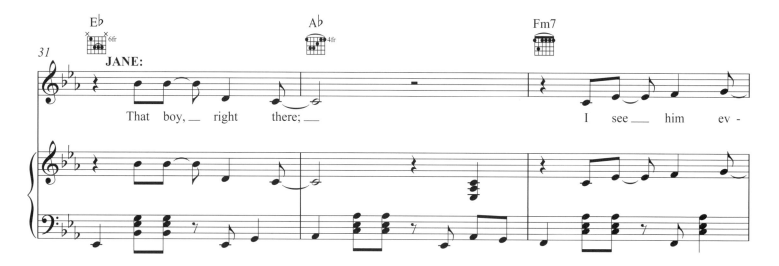

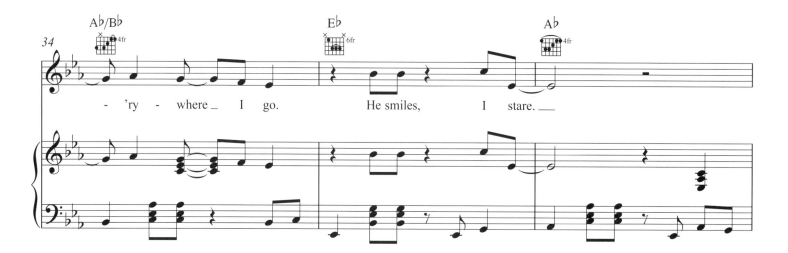

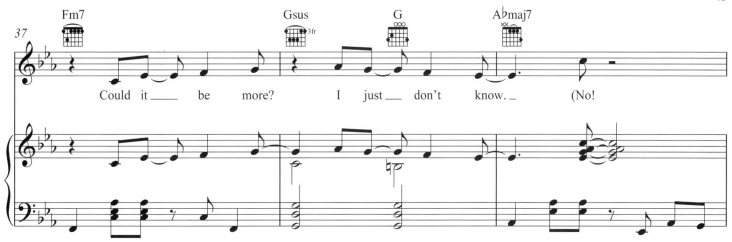

Could it ___ be more? I just ___ don't know. ___ (No!

Don't be stu - pid.) Told my - self ___ a mil - lion times ___ be - fore. ___

___ (No! Don't be fool - ish.) He is not ___ your kind

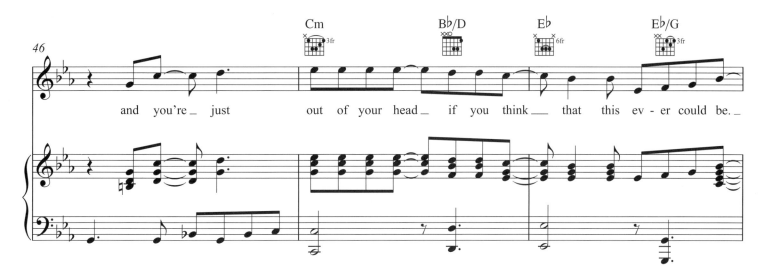

and you're ___ just out of your head ___ if you think ___ that this ev - er could be. ___

-pen to guys like me. (No!) (No!)

Things like this ___ don't hap - pen. ___

Things like this ___ don't hap - pen. ___

rit.

Moderately slow, expressively

CALOGERO:

And then she's there. The chance will nev - er come ___ a - gain.

NICKY MACHIAVELLI

Music by ALAN MENKEN
Lyrics by GLENN SLATER

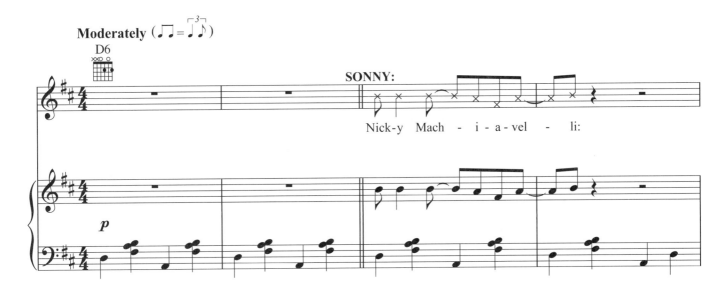

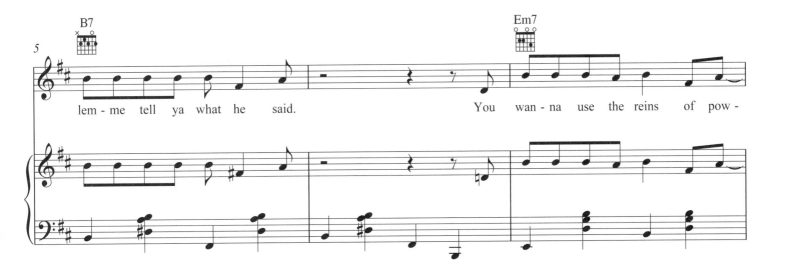

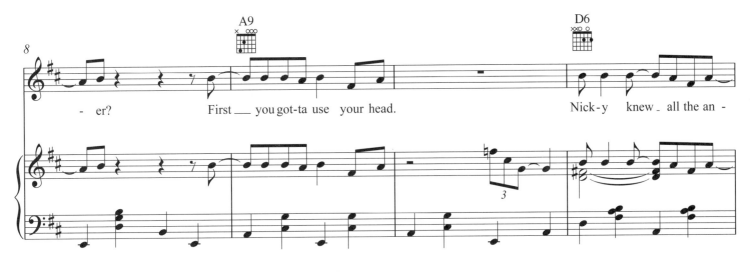

-gles. Nick-y laid it out real clear. You

got-ta choose fear or love, __ kid. Ya got-ta choose love or _____

__ fear. Nick-y's num-ber one se - cret was _

__ a - vail - a - bil - i - ty. That's _ why I'm here _ on this cor-

-ness looks a lot like weak - ness, e - ven when you spread it thick.

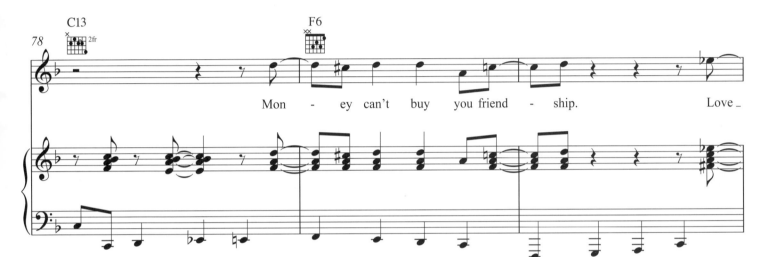

Mon - ey can't buy you friend - ship. Love __

__ can al - ways dis - ap - pear. But fear __ is cash __ in the bank, __

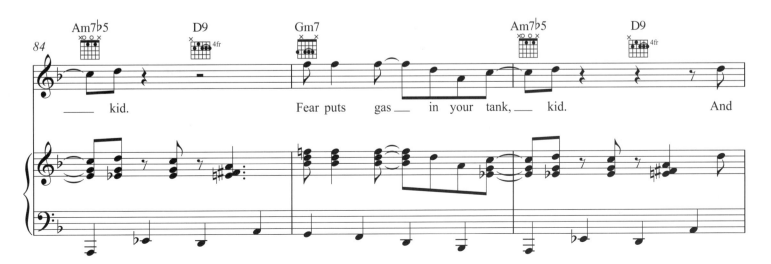

__ kid. Fear puts gas __ in your tank, __ kid. And

kid, but you live with what you choose. Nick-y told me his se-

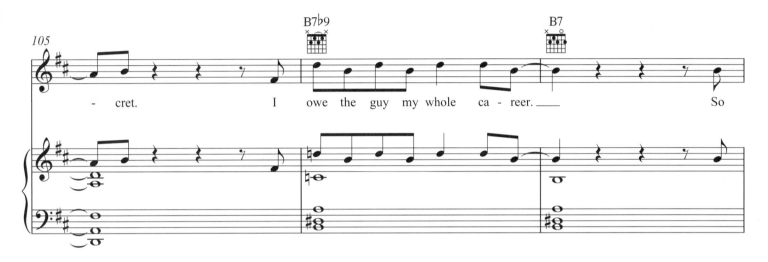

-cret. I owe the guy my whole ca-reer. So

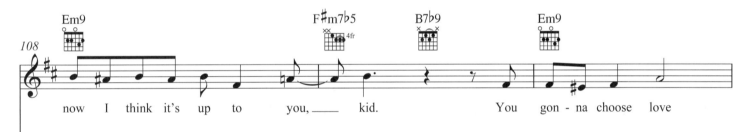

now I think it's up to you, kid. You gon-na choose love

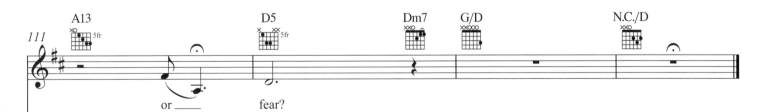

or fear?

THESE STREETS

Music by ALAN MENKEN
Lyrics by GLENN SLATER

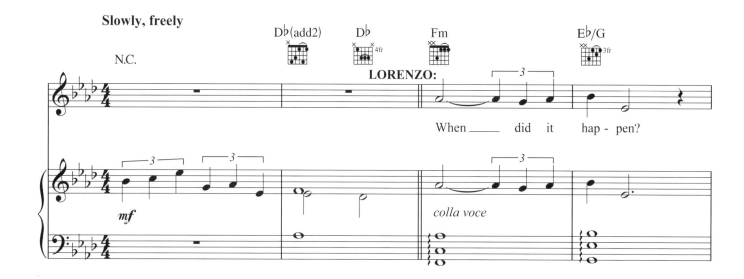

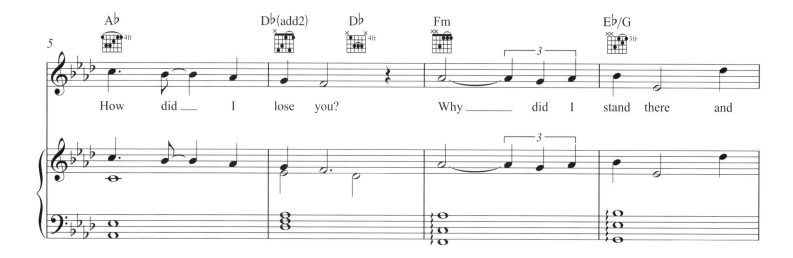

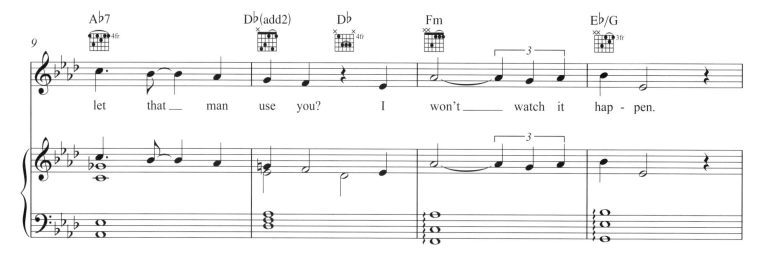

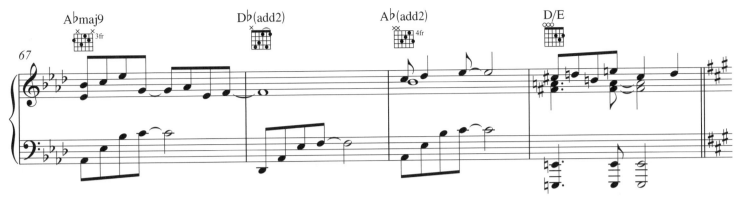

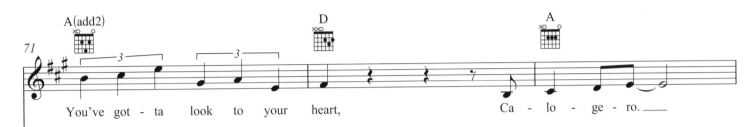

You've got - ta look to your heart, Ca - lo - ge - ro. ___

Don't you get trapped _ here, be smart, Ca -

lo - ge - ro.   Ca - lo - ge - ro...!   These

rall.

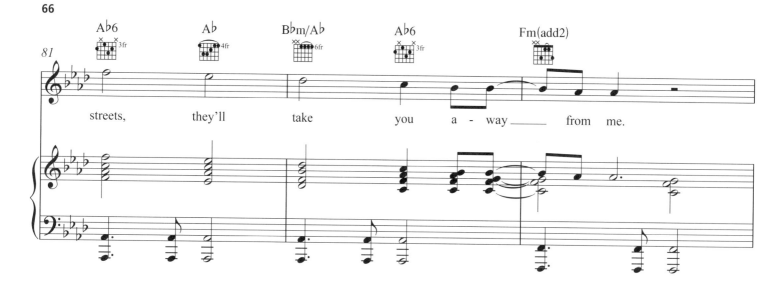

streets, they'll take you a - way ___ from me.

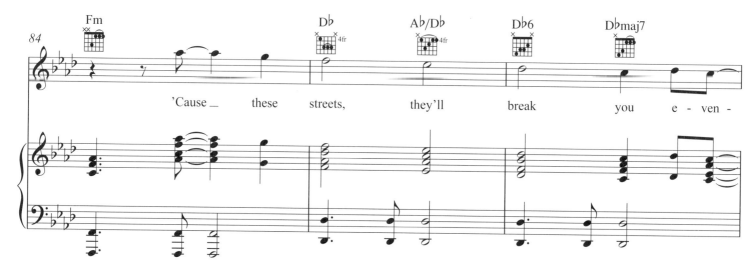

'Cause ___ these streets, they'll break you e - ven -

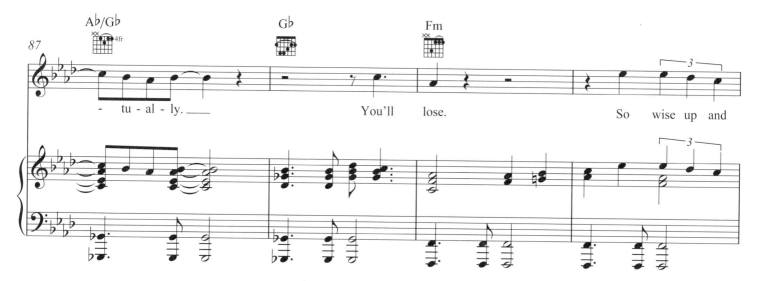

- tu - al - ly. ___ You'll lose. So wise up and

choose. ___ Re - mem - ber the prom - ise you made, ___

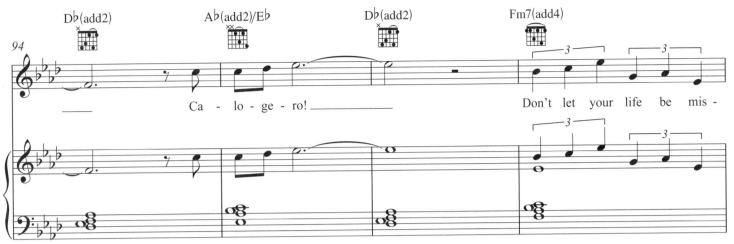

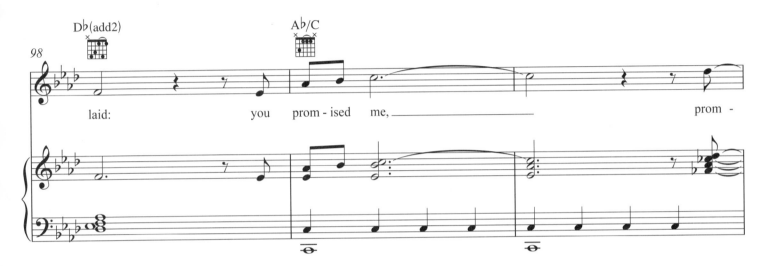

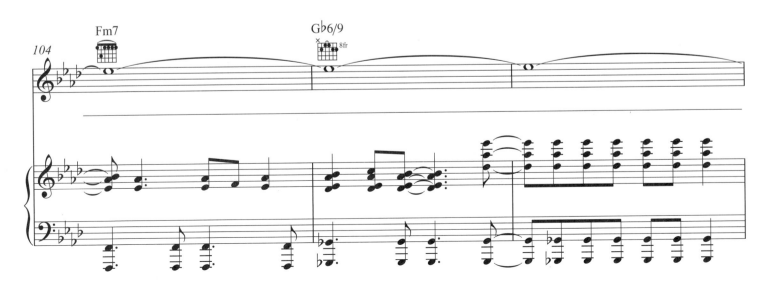

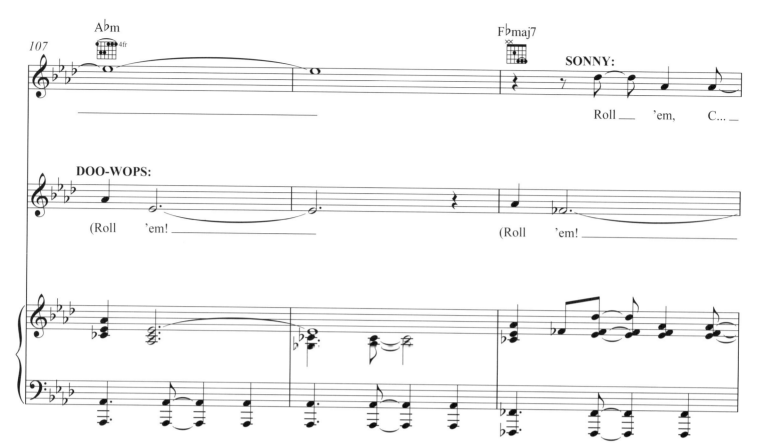

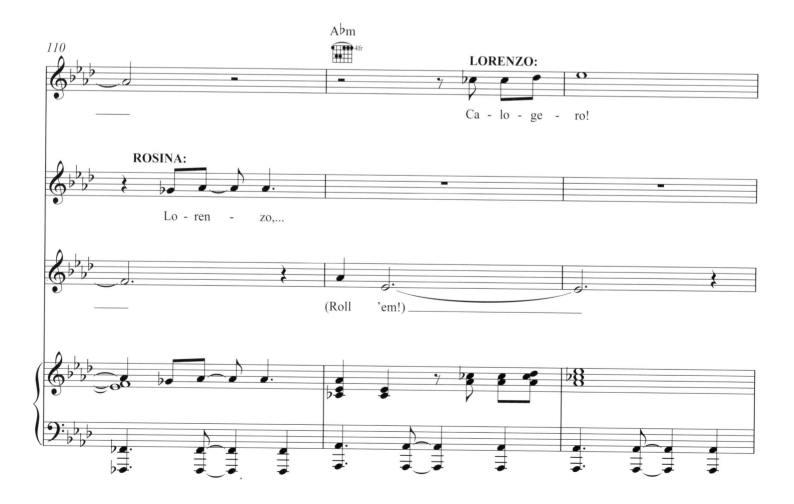

ONE OF THE GREAT ONES

Music by ALAN MENKEN
Lyrics by GLENN SLATER

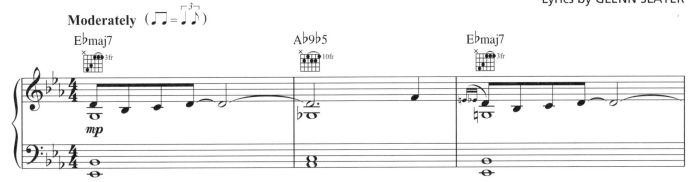

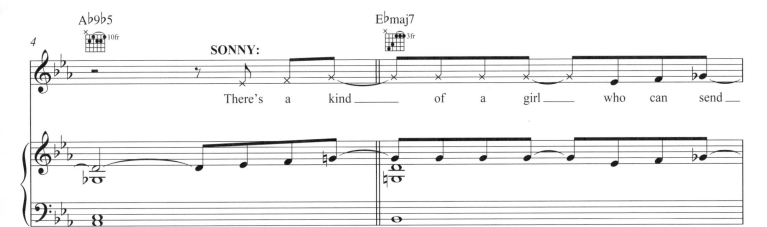

SONNY:
There's a kind ____ of a girl ____ who can send ____

____ your heart whirl-ing a - way. ____ But

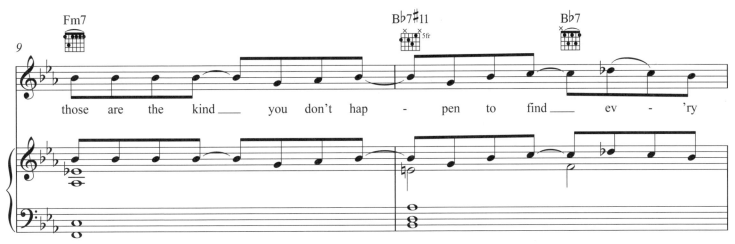

those are the kind ____ you don't hap - pen to find ____ ev - 'ry

72

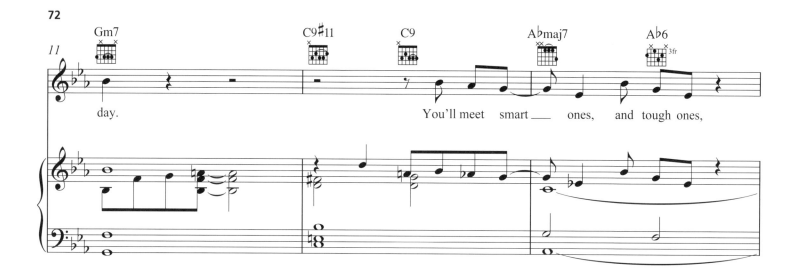

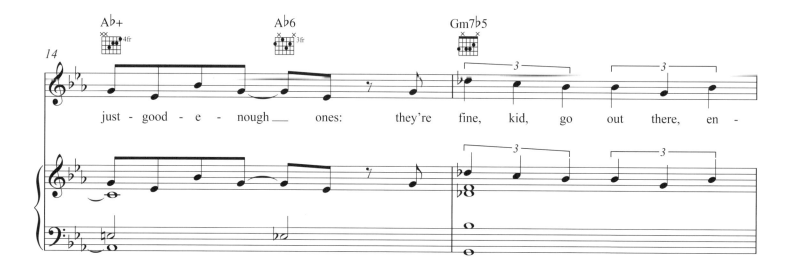

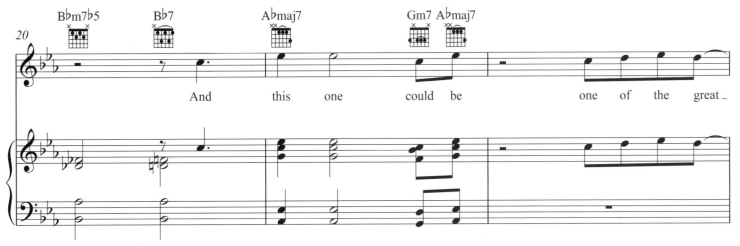

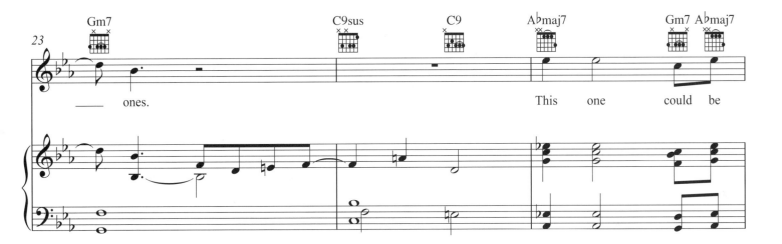

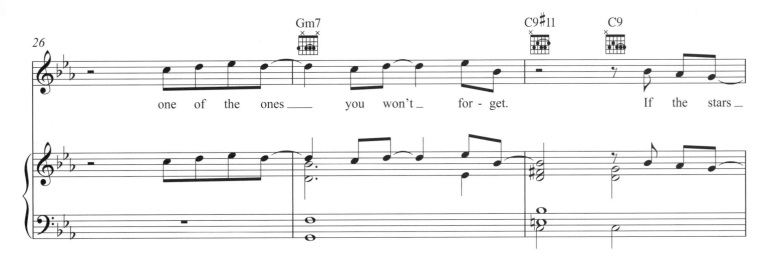

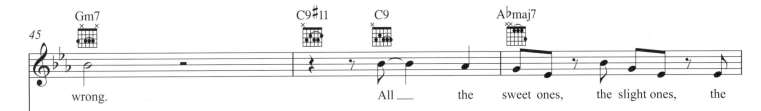

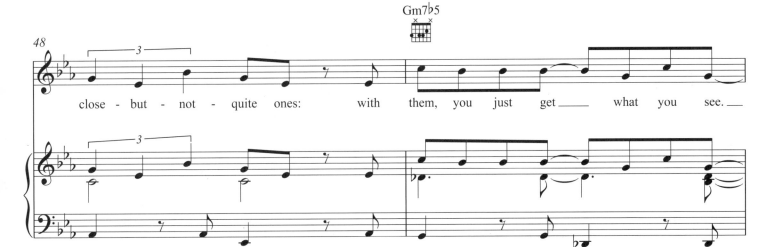

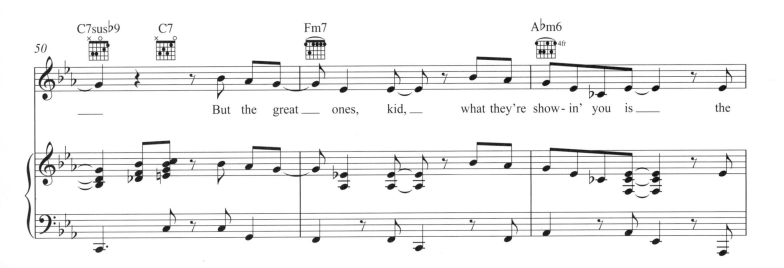

man you could be. _____ And this girl could be

one of the great ___ ones.

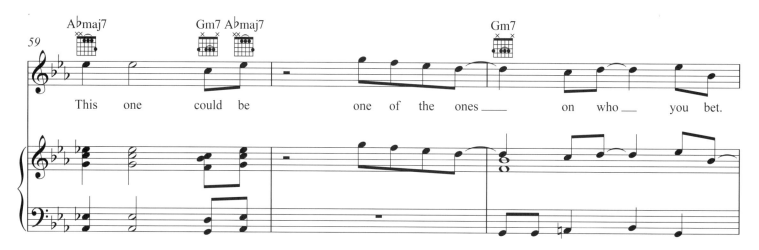

This one could be one of the ones ___ on who ___ you bet.

Do you fly ___ off the rails ___ with the wind ___ in your sails when-

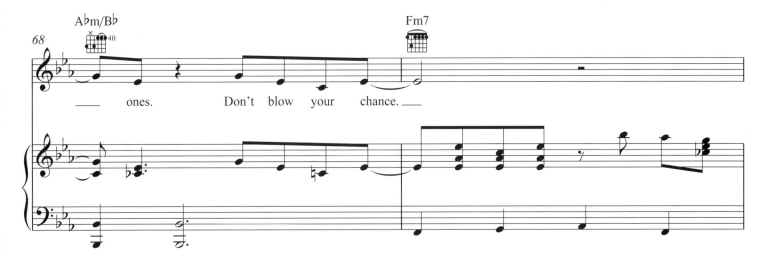

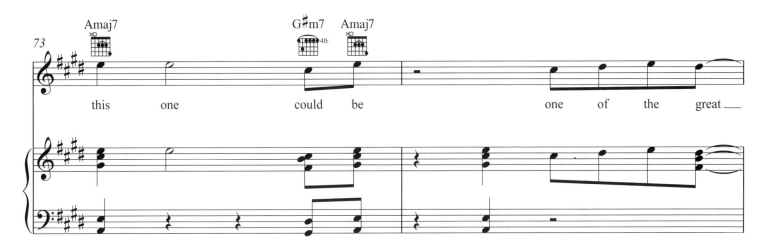

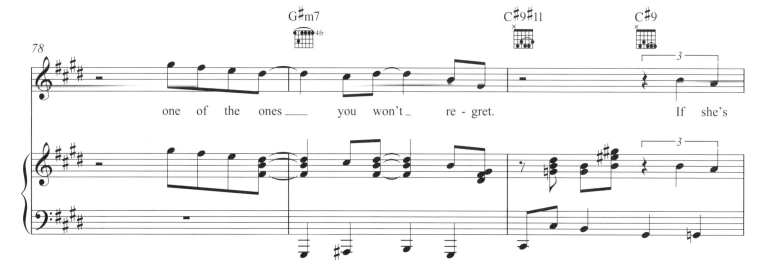

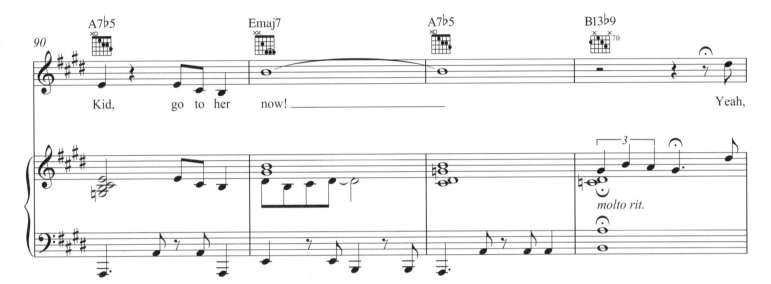

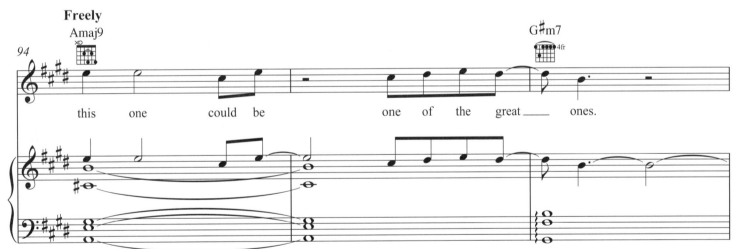

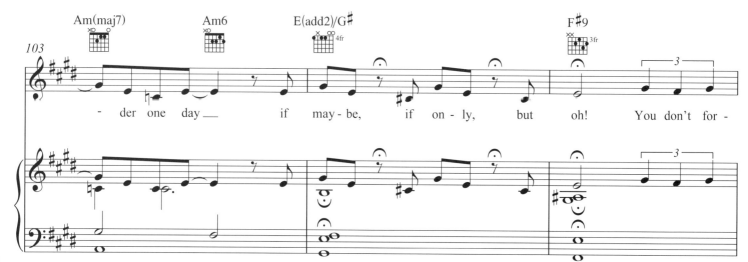

HURT SOMEONE

Music by ALAN MENKEN
Lyrics by GLENN SLATER

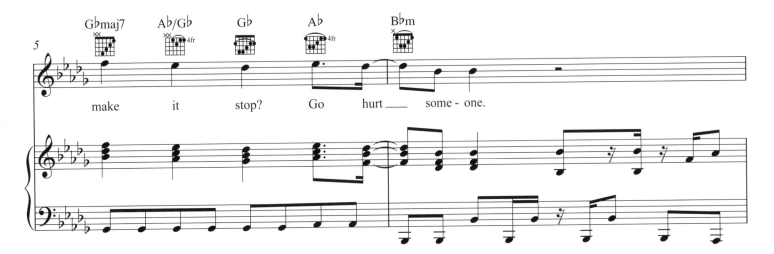

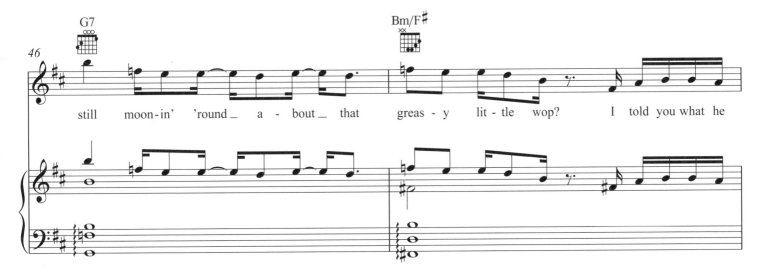

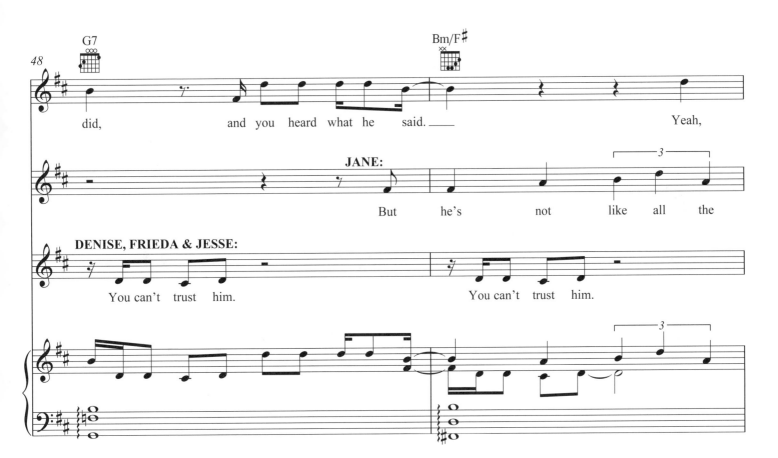

e - ven tho' __ he tried __ to get the oth - er ones __ to stop, I'm in the

rest.

mood to go __ and hurt some - one, and he's the one! __

JANE:

Knew he was - n't like __ that, de -

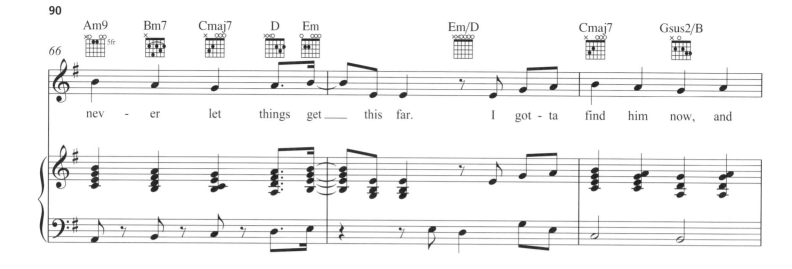

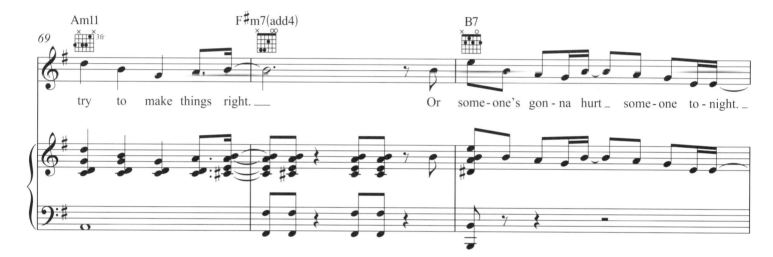

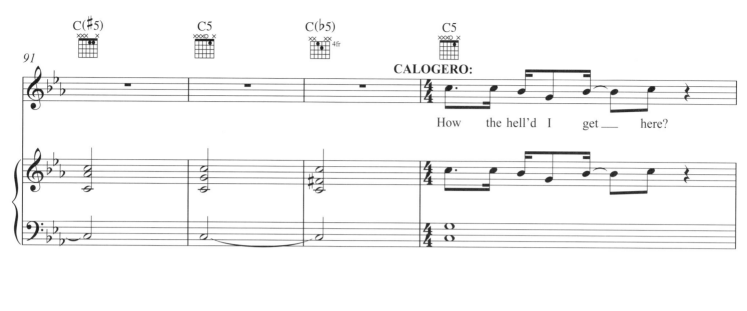

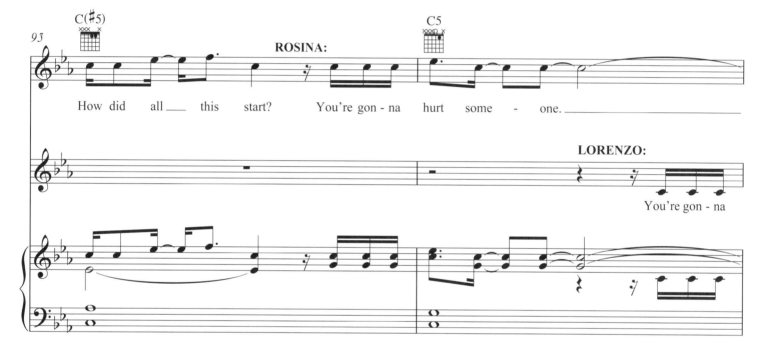

hurt some - one. _____ Some - how I

CALOGERO:

LORENZO:

You're gon - na hurt some - one. ___

lost my way and lost ___ my ___ mind, un - til I

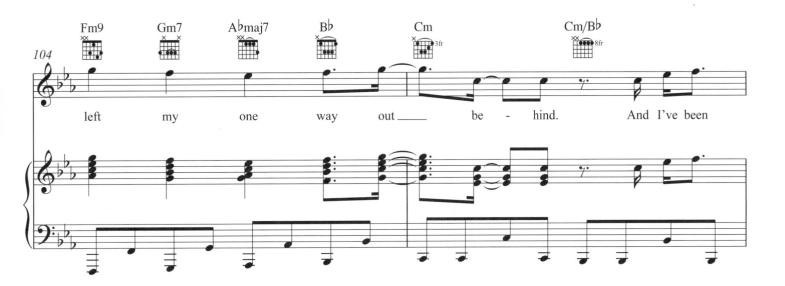

left my one way out ___ be - hind. And I've been

IN A WORLD LIKE THIS

Music by ALAN MENKEN
Lyrics by GLENN SLATER

Well, let 'em talk, talk, talk; who cares what they say? _

Now that you're here, ___ well, it's clear - er than day ___ that those words, _

JANE:

Those words, _ no, no, ___ not me, ___

___ they're not true. ___ They're not me, _____ they're not you! _

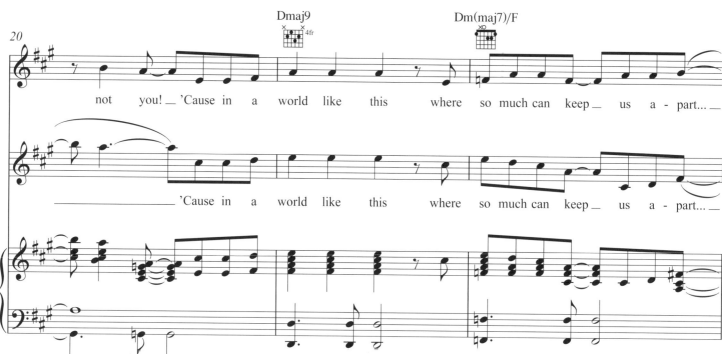

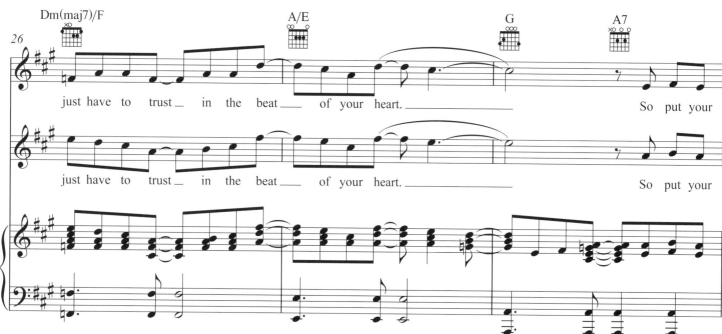

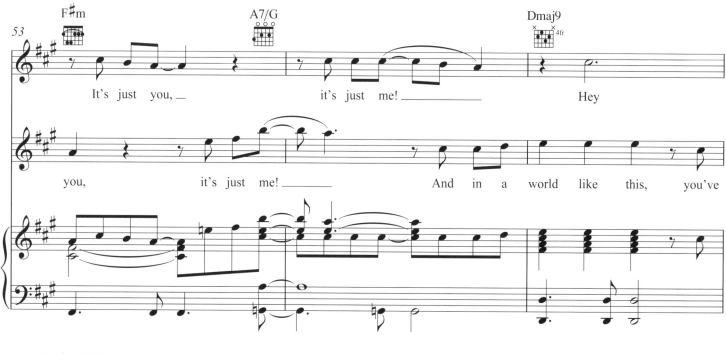

THE CHOICES WE MAKE

Music by ALAN MENKEN
Lyrics by GLENN SLATER

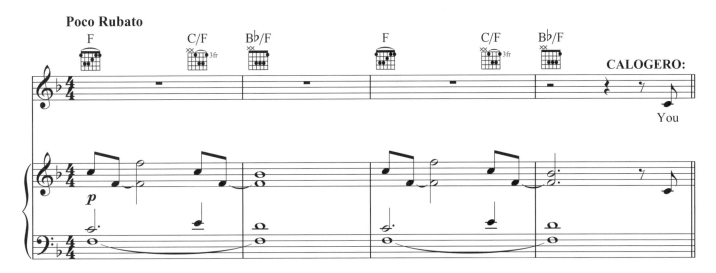

CALOGERO:

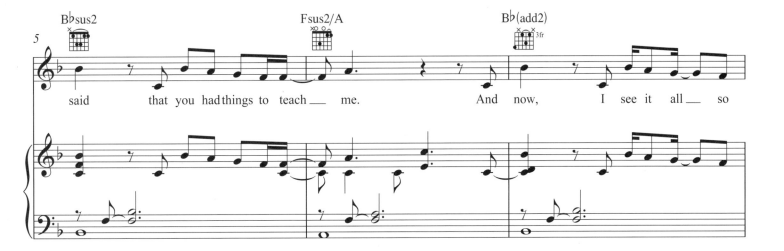

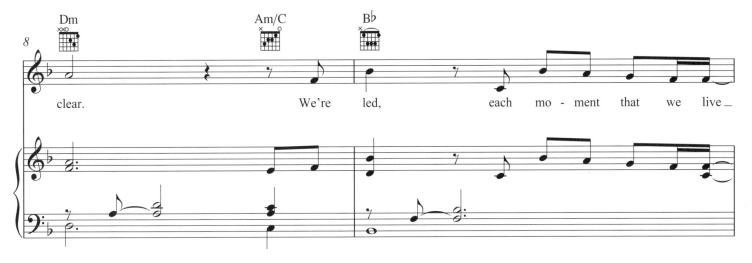

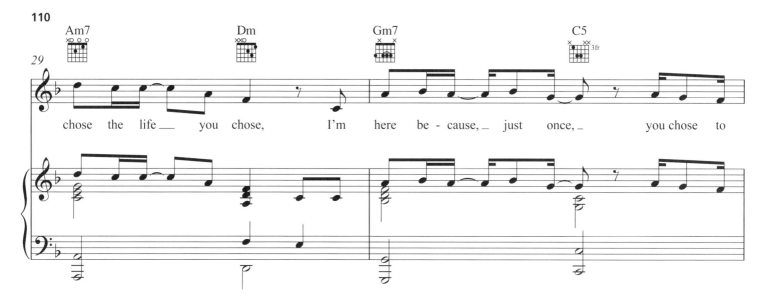

chose the life ___ you chose, I'm here be - cause, ___ just once, ___ you chose to

love. And now your whole life lies be - fore ___

LORENZO:

___ you. It's time that you be - come a man. ___ You'll know

how: just look at what's in - side ___ you, and ___ let your tal - ent guide ___

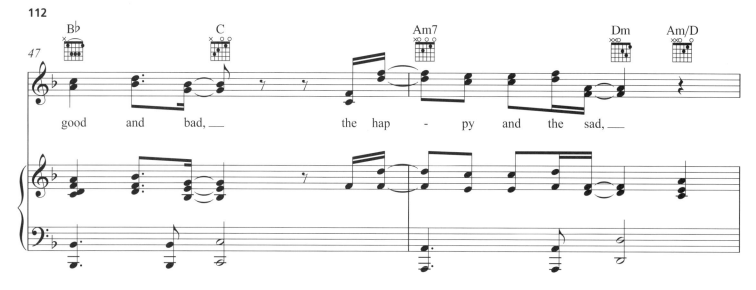

good and bad, ___ the hap - py and the sad, ___

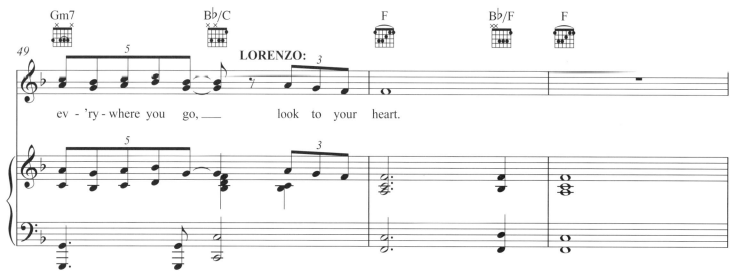

ev - 'ry - where you go, ___ look to your heart.

LORENZO:

This is a Bronx tale, ___ it's just an - oth - er

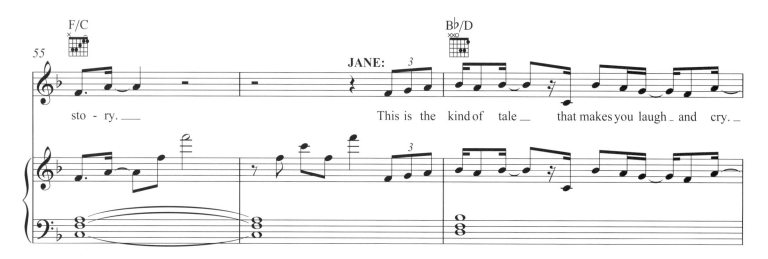

sto - ry. ___ This is the kind of tale ___ that makes you laugh ___ and cry. ___

JANE:

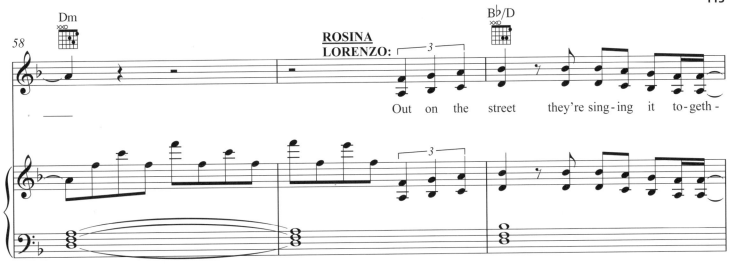

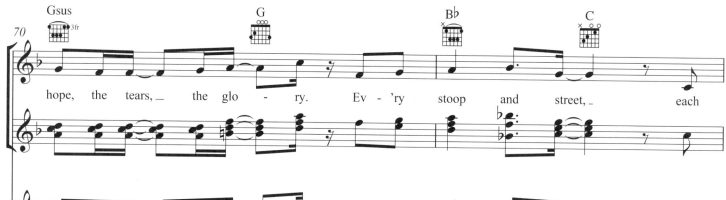

win and each de-feat, __ the sin-ners and the saints, __ the sweet __

__ and bit-ter - sweet. __ And when the tale's com - plete, __ you've

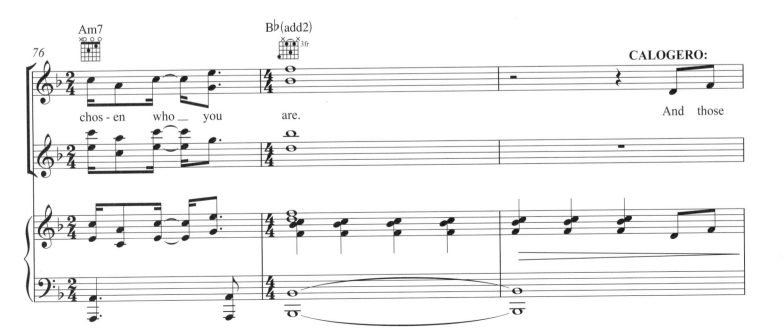

chos - en who __ you are.

CALOGERO:

And those

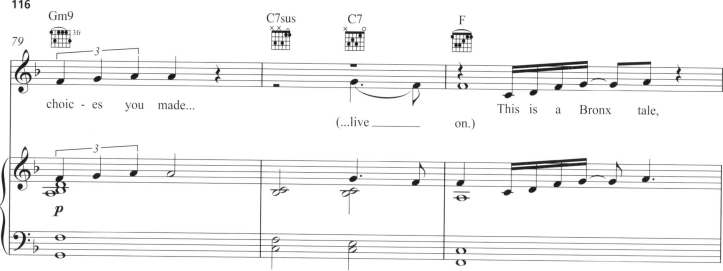

choic - es you made...
(...live _____ on.)
This is a Bronx tale,

and that's my sto - ry, the world I lived _ in, the peo - ple I knew. _

It's just a Bronx _ tale, and like they all do, it

PIANO/VOCAL SELECTIONS

TOMMY MOTTOLA   THE DODGERS
TRIBECA PRODUCTIONS
EVAMERE ENTERTAINMENT   NEIGHBORHOOD FILMS
JEFFREY SINE   COHEN PRIVATE VENTURES   GRANT JOHNSON
in association with PAPER MILL PLAYHOUSE
present

A BRONX TALE

Book by
CHAZZ PALMINTERI

Music by
ALAN MENKEN

Lyrics by
GLENN SLATER

Based on the Play by CHAZZ PALMINTERI

with

NICK CORDERO

RICHARD H. BLAKE   BOBBY CONTE THORNTON

ARIANA DEBOSE   LUCIA GIANNETTA   BRADLEY GIBSON   HUDSON LOVERRO

MICHELLE ARAVENA   GILBERT L. BAILEY II   JOE BARBARA   MICHAEL BARRA   JONATHAN BRODY   TED BRUNETTI
GERALD CAESAR   BRITTANY CONIGATTI   KALEIGH CRONIN   TRISTA DOLLISON   DAVID MICHAEL GARRY   RORY MAX KAPLAN
CHARLIE MARCUS   DOMINIC NOLFI   WONU OGUNFOWORA   CHRISTIANI PITTS   PAUL SALVATORIELLO   JOEY SORGE
ATHAN SPOREK   JOSEPH J. SIMEONE   CARY TEDDER   KIRSTIN TUCKER   KEITH WHITE

Scenic Design **BEOWULF BORITT**	Costume Design **WILLIAM IVEY LONG**	Lighting Design **HOWELL BINKLEY**	Sound Design **GARETH OWEN**
Hair and Wig Design **PAUL HUNTLEY**	Makeup Design **ANNE FORD-COATES**	Fight Coordinator **ROBERT WESTLEY**	Technical Supervision **HUDSON THEATRICAL ASSOCIATES**
Orchestrations **DOUG BESTERMAN**	Music Direction **JONATHAN SMITH**	Period Music Consultant **JOHNNY GALE**	Music Coordinator **JOHN MILLER**
Associate Director **STEPHEN EDLUND**	Associate Choreographer **MARC KIMELMAN**	Company Manager **MIGUEL A. ORTIZ**	Production Stage Manager **BEVERLY JENKINS**
Casting **TARA RUBIN CASTING** **MERRI SUGARMAN, CSA**	Press Representative **BONEAU/BRYAN-BROWN**	Advertising/Marketing **AKA**	Promotions **RED RISING MARKETING**

Associate Producer
LAUREN MITCHELL

Executive Producer
SALLY CAMPBELL MORSE

General Management
DODGER MANAGEMENT GROUP

Music Supervision and Arrangements by
RON MELROSE

Choreography by
SERGIO TRUJILLO

Direction by
ROBERT DE NIRO AND JERRY ZAKS

World Premiere, Paper Mill Playhouse, in Milburn, New Jersey on February 14, 2016
Mark S. Hoebee, Artistic Director, Todd Schmidt, Managing Director

The Producers wish to express their appreciation to Theatre Developent Fund for its support of this production.

ISBN 978-1-5400-1242-5

7777 W. BLUEMOUND RD. P.O. BOX 13819 MILWAUKEE, WI 53213

In Australia Contact:
Hal Leonard Australia Pty. Ltd.
4 Lentara Court
Cheltenham, Victoria, 3192 Australia
Email: ausadmin@halleonard.com.au

Visit Hal Leonard Online at
www.halleonard.com